History Of Zimbabwe For Kids

A History Series

Children Explore Histories Of The World Edition

BABY PROFESSOR

EDUCATION KIDS

Speedy Publishing LLC
40 E. Main St. #1156
Newark, DE 19711
www.speedypublishing.com

The name "Zimbabwe" is derived from two words of Shona language 'dzimba' ('houses') and 'mabwe' ('stones') and can be translated into English as 'Big houses of stones' or 'honorable houses'.

L. Kariba

Maramba
O

Binga
o

ZIMB

Bulawa

Maun

BOTSWANA

Zimbabwe was formerly known as Southern Rhodesia, Rhodesia and Zimbabwe Rhodesia (named after South African businessman Cecil Rhodes).

In 1000 AD, Shona people began their rule and built a city called Zimbabwe.

In 1400s, Karanga branch of the Shona established the Mwanamutapa Empire.

By 1500,
Christianity was
introduced by
the Portuguese
explorers.

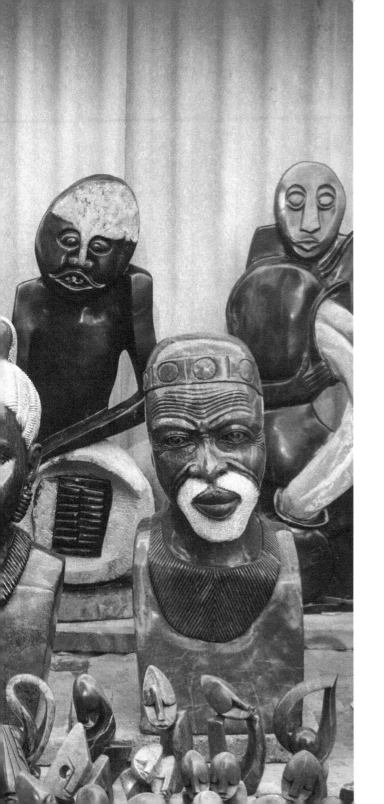

Lobengula, the ruler, signed an agreement that granted mineral rights to the British South African Company in 1888.

The British South African Company occupied the region and called the territory Rhodesia by 1893.

UNIVERSAL POST

1874
1949

NORTHERN
RHODESIA

Great Britain recognized southern and northern Rhodesia as separate territories.

Southern Rhodesia became a self-governing British Colony by 1923.

In 1953, Great Britain set up the Federation of Rhodesia and Nyasaland, which included the territories of Southern and Northern Rhodesia.

It was 1963 when the Federation of Rhodesia and Nyasaland was dissolved.

A year after, Northern Rhodesia became Zambia and Southern Rhodesia became known as Rhodesia.

November 11, 1965, Prime Minister, Ian Smith, declared Rhodesia independent. Great Britain declared this action illegal and banned trade with Rhodesia.

Then the United Nations imposed sanctions on Rhodesia in 1966.

In 1969, a new constitution was introduced to prevent black Africans from ever gaining control of the government.

In 1970-1974, the Civil War between government troops and black guerrillas began.

From 1977-1979 Prime Minister Smith began to make plans to establish a new government with a majority of black leaders.

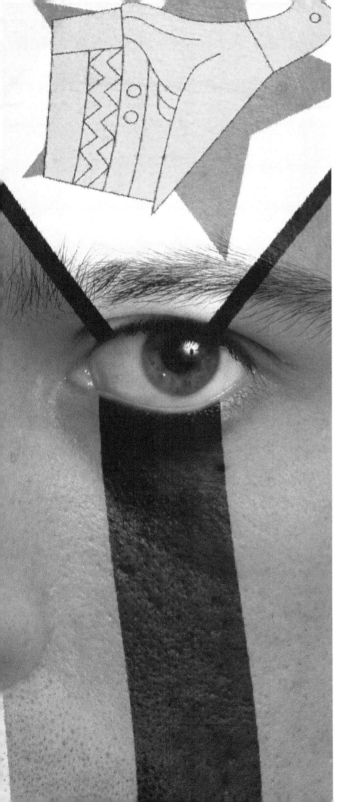

It was by April 18, 1980, when Great Britain recognized the country's independence and Rhodesia's name was officially changed to Zimbabwe.

The History of Zimbabwe is very rich, research and learn more!

Visit

BABY PROFESSOR
EDUCATION KIDS

www.BabyProfessorBooks.com

to download Free Baby Professor eBooks
and view our catalog of new and exciting
Children's Books

CPSIA information can be obtained
at www.ICGtesting.com
Printed in the USA
LVHW050720070622
720660LV00007B/322